Cover Photo: Midwest Floods, July 1993 - Homes, businesses, and personal property were all destroyed by the high flood levels. Courtesy of Andrea Booher, FEMA.

Emergency Action Planning for State Regulated High-Hazard Potential Dams

Findings, Recommendations, and Strategies

October 2006

Prepared by the National Dam Safety Review Board
Task Group on Emergency Action Planning and Response

TABLE OF CONTENTS

EXECUTIVE SUMMARY

An Emergency Action Plan (EAP) is one of the primary safeguards against the loss of life and property damage that can result from the failure of a high-hazard potential dam. Today, there are approximately 8,300 state-regulated high-hazard potential dams in the United States. Of these 8.300 dams, approximately 40 percent do not have an EAP.

Since the establishment of the National Dam Safety Program in 1979, both the state and federal sectors have made significant progress in increasing the number of state-regulated high-hazard potential dams with EAP's. The dam safety community recognizes, however, that much more must be done to reach the goal established in January 2006 by the National Dam Safety Review Board: achieve 100 percent compliance for EAP's for high-hazard potential dams.

When the National Dam Safety Review Board met in October 2005, the losses from Hurricane Katrina had just exposed significant failures in all aspects of the Nation's emergency mitigation, planning, and response. The failure of the emergency management system to respond quickly and effectively to the disaster brought to the forefront the need for all hazard areas, including dam safety, to refocus their attention on this critical requirement. For the dam infrastructure, the need for emergency action planning is heightened by the aging of dams in the United States. The 2005 *Report Card for America's Infrastructure* (American Society of Civil Engineers, March 2005) states that the number of unsafe or deficient dams in the United States has risen by more than 33 percent since 1998, to more than 3,500.

To address these issues, the National Dam Safety Review Board established the Task Group on Emergency Action Planning and Response. The Task Group, which began its work in January 2006, recognized that the success of its effort would require the involvement of all of the sectors with an interest in its outcome. As a result, the sectors represented on the Task Group include state and federal dam safety professionals and engineers, the emergency management community, the security and protection community, and emergency response organizations. Appendix D includes the list of Task Group members.

This document provides the Task Group's findings, recommendations, and strategies for significantly increasing the number of EAP's for state-regulated high-hazard potential dams. [1] The six findings of the Task Group are:

- Finding #1: Communication and Coordination between Dam Safety Officials, Dam Owners, and Emergency Responders Can Be Improved

- Finding #2: The Effects of Dam Failures Must Be Better Communicated

- Finding #3: The EAP Document Can Be Improved

- Finding #4: Non-Federal High-Hazard Potential Classification Dams Must be Mapped for Dam Breach

- Finding #5: Some States Do Not Require EAP's for High-Hazard Potential Classification Dams

- Finding #6: There are Limited Funds for Emergency Action Planning for Dams

---

[1] Although the focus of this document is on high-hazard potential dams, the findings, recommendations, and strategies also apply to significant-hazard potential dams.

For each of the six findings, the Task Group developed a number of recommendations for implementing the findings by a cross-section of stakeholders, including policymakers, state and local dam safety officials, dam owners, and state and local emergency managers and emergency responders. The findings and recommendations are presented in Section II.

The Task Group also considered a number of issues affecting emergency action planning for dams, such as institutional barriers to communication, best processes for communication, responsibilities of emergency responders, and interagency coordination of EAP exercises. The strategies and best practices to address these issues are included in Appendix A. Appendix B includes data from the Dam Safety Program Management Tools (DSPMT) on current emergency action planning by the states. The performance measure on emergency action planning for high-hazard potential classification dams that was adopted by the National Dam Safety Review Board at its January 2006 meeting is included in Appendix C.

I. OVERVIEW

A. Purpose and Scope

The purpose of this document is to provide findings, recommendations, and strategies for significantly increasing the number of Emergency Action Plans (EAP's) for state-regulated high-hazard potential dams. The recommendations and strategies can be implemented by a cross-section of stakeholders, including policymakers, state and local dam safety officials, dam owners, and state and local emergency managers and emergency responders.

This section of the document describes the goals and the work of the National Dam Safety Review Board (Review Board) Task Group on Emergency Action Planning and Response (Task Group) and provides an overview of the current status of emergency action planning by the states. Section II presents the findings and recommendations of the Task Group. Appendix A provides strategies and best practices to assist the states in all aspects of the emergency action planning process for high-hazard potential dams. Appendix B presents data from the Dam Safety Program Management Tools on current emergency action planning by the states. Appendix C includes the performance measure on emergency action planning for high-hazard potential dams that was adopted by the Review Board at its January 2006 meeting.

B. Task Group on Emergency Action Planning and Response

The devastating losses resulting from Hurricane Katrina exposed significant failures in all aspects of the Nation's emergency mitigation, planning, and response. In particular, the failure of the emergency management system to respond quickly and effectively to the disaster brought to the forefront the need for all hazard areas, including dam safety, to refocus attention on this critical requirement.

The dam safety community recognizes that comprehensive emergency management planning is the most effective approach to emergency management at all levels of government. However, about 40 percent of the Nation's state-regulated high-hazard potential dams currently do not have an EAP to be used in the event of a dam failure resulting from a natural event, such as a large storm or earthquake, or from a manmade event, such as a terrorist attack. [2] EAP's are essential because they identify the area below the dam that would be flooded from a failure, establish the communication between the dam owner and emergency response personnel, provide for notification and evacuations conducted by police, fire, and rescue teams, and predict the timing of the dambreak floodwave. It is essential that first responders have critical emergency action planning information to effect safe and successful evacuations, save lives, and help keep responders out of danger.

The Review Board, which was authorized under Public Law 104-303 and Public Law 107-310, monitors the safety and security of dams in the United States; advises the Director of the Federal Emergency Management Agency (FEMA) on national dam safety policy; consults with the Director of FEMA for the purpose of establishing and maintaining a coordinated National Dam Safety Program; determines with the Director of FEMA the amount of funds to be distributed to the states under the Dam Safety and Security Act of 2002 (Act); and monitors state implementation of the assistance program. Work Groups established under the Review Board assist the Director of FEMA and the Review Board in carrying out the requirements of the Act.

---

[2] Although approximately one-half of the Nation's state-regulated high-hazard potential classification dams have an EAP, some of these EAP's may be outdated or may not have been recently exercised.

The bylaws for the Review Board state that *ad hoc* Task Groups may be established to address specific issues that arise in dam safety. In response to the issues raised by Hurricane Katrina, the Review Board established the Task Group at its October 2005 meeting. The goals of the Task Group, which began its work in January 2006, were to review the state of emergency action planning in the dam sector and to develop recommendations and strategies for significantly increasing the number of state-regulated high-hazard potential dams in the United States with EAP's.

The Task Group acknowledges that the success of its effort to significantly increase the number of state-regulated high-hazard potential dams requires the involvement of all of the sectors with an interest in its outcome. These sectors include state and federal dam safety professionals and engineers, dam owners, the emergency management community, the security and protection community, emergency response organizations, including the National Weather Service (NWS) and the DHS Directorate for Preparedness (PREP), and other interested stakeholders. (Appendix D includes the list of Task Group members.)

C. Emergency Action Planning by the States

In the currently published National Inventory of Dams (NID), there are approximately 79,500 dams in the United States, including about 11,800 dams that are considered "high hazard," meaning that their failure will likely result in loss of life and significant downstream property damage. The NID indicates that at least 63,000 of the dams are state regulated (incomplete data fields prevent a more exact figure). Approximately 4,500 dams are regulated by federal agencies, and the remaining dams are not regulated by any government agency.

The U.S. Army Corps of Engineers (USACE), Dam Safety Program Management Tools (DSPMT) provides the following data from 2005/2006 on non-federal, state-regulated high-hazard potential dams:

- State dam inventories contain 8,313 non-federal state-regulated high-hazard potential classification dams.

- Of these 8,313 dams, 4,057 (49 percent) have an EAP; 3,356 (40 percent) do not have an EAP; and 726 (9 percent) do not require an EAP. [3]

Appendix B includes detailed data from the DSPMT on the current status of emergency action planning by the states. The data in Appendix B is drawn from responses provided by the states to the combined Review Board/Association of State Dam Safety Officials (ASDSO) questions in 2005 for the 2004 reporting year, and from updated inventory information to the NID provided in 2005/2006.

---

[3] The data does not total 100 percent because 122 non-federal state-regulated high-hazard potential dams (1.5 percent) have a blank value for EAP. The states have not provided a clear rationale in their responses to Review Board or ASDSO questions as to why the EAP values are blank for these dams or why EAP's are indicated as not required for the 9 percent high-hazard potential dams not requiring an EAP.

II. FINDINGS AND RECOMMENDATIONS

The dam safety community recognizes that comprehensive emergency management planning is the most effective approach to emergency management at all levels of government. An Emergency Action Plan (EAP) is essential for dam owners and first responders in the event of a dam failure resulting from a natural event, such as a large storm or earthquake, from an accident, or from a manmade event, such as a terrorist attack.

This section presents the findings and recommendations of the National Dam Safety Review Board (Review Board) Task Group on Emergency Action Planning and Response (Task Group) on the issues that are impacting the implementation of EAP's for state-regulated high-hazard potential classification dams. As noted in Section I, the Task Group recognizes that a significant number of the recommendations can be implemented by a cross-section of sectors and stakeholders.

A. Finding #1: Communication and Coordination between Dam Safety Officials, Dam Owners, and Emergency Responders Can Be Improved

The Task Group identified a number of issues pertaining to the institutional relationships between dam safety officials, dam owners, and emergency responders that affect emergency action planning for dams. The Task Group found that issues of awareness, time and resources, and information overload, e.g., multiple, voluminous EAP's, are important factors in the ability and willingness of stakeholders in the dam safety community to implement and exercise EAP's. The Task Group also acknowledged the importance of recognizing that the EAP for a dam is one part of the larger community emergency response plan.

Recommendations:

1. Develop partnerships and exercises with emergency managers and responders at the various levels of government who would be involved in an emergency incident at dams within their jurisdictions.

   Stakeholders: State and federal dam safety officials; dam owners; emergency managers and responders

2. Establish a local, county-wide dam safety day during which an exercise of an EAP is conducted on a high-hazard potential classification dam.

   Stakeholders: Policymakers; state and federal dam safety officials; emergency managers and responders

3. Consolidate EAP exercises on a county-wide or watershed basis to more efficiently utilize the time and resources of officials

   Stakeholders: State and federal dam safety officials; dam owners; emergency managers and responders

4. Promote annual meetings between dam owners and emergency managers to facilitate understanding of the EAP. During the meetings, the dam owner should explain the EAP, pre-planned emergency procedures, and inundation maps to ensure the emergency managers understand the plan. During the meetings, the emergency managers also can determine which sections of the EAP are applicable to their role and tailor the document to better meet their needs, *i.e.*, sections not applicable to the emergency manager's mission can be deleted.

   Stakeholders: FEMA; Review Board; Association of State Dam Safety Officials (ASDSO); state and federal dam safety officials; dam owners; emergency managers and responders

5. Promote EAP's that are specific to each dam and formatted for ease of use. A sample EAP was recently developed by ASDSO and the U.S. Department of Agriculture, Natural Resources Conservation Service (NRCS).

   Stakeholders: FEMA; Review Board; ASDSO; state and federal dam safety officials; dam owners; emergency managers and responders

6. Tie in the exercise of an EAP for a high-hazard potential dam with other scheduled exercises, such as hurricane drills.

   Stakeholders: State and federal dam safety officials; emergency managers and responders; Department Homeland Security (DHS) Directorate of Preparedness (PREP)

B. Finding #2: The Effects of Dam Failures Must Be Better Communicated

In the event of a dam failure, the potential energy of the water stored behind even a small dam is capable of causing loss of life, great property damage, and an extended period of denial of the services that dams provide. The Task Group found that there is a lack of awareness of the effects of a dam failure outside of the dam safety community.

Recommendations:

1. Develop partnerships and exercises with the floodplain managers, emergency management officials, dam owner communities, and other stakeholders to enhance the understanding of the need for EAP's for high-hazard potential dams.

   Stakeholders: FEMA; Review Board; ASDSO; state and federal dam safety officials; National Emergency Management Agency (NEMA); American Society of Civil Engineers (ASCE); National Watershed Coalition; Association of State Floodplain Managers (ASFPM); Johnstown and other National Park Service (NPS) memorial sites; Lake Management Associations; and news organizations

2. Promote existing awareness and educational products and develop new awareness and educational products for the public and professionals on the need for emergency action planning for dams as an effective mitigation strategy for natural hazards, accidents, or manmade incidents.

   Stakeholders: FEMA; Review Board; ASDSO; state and federal dam safety officials; PREP; NEMA; ASCE; National Watershed Coalition; ASFPM; Johnstown and other NPS memorial sites; Lake Management Associations; and news organizations

3. Leverage relationships with dam safety organizations to promote dam safety awareness.

   Stakeholders: FEMA; Review Board; ASDSO; state and federal dam safety officials; PREP; NEMA; ASCE; National Watershed Coalition; ASFPM; Johnstown and other NPS memorial sites; Lake Management Associations; and news organizations

4. Make better use of the media and the Internet for disseminating information on the effects of dam failures resulting from natural hazards, accidents, or manmade incidents.

   Stakeholders: FEMA; Review Board; ASDSO; state and federal dam safety officials; PREP; NEMA; ASCE; National Watershed Coalition; ASFPM; Johnstown and other NPS memorial sites; Lake Management Associations; and news organizations

5. Make education and awareness of dam safety occur on a regular basis, such as through locally-sponsored hazard/dam safety days.

   Stakeholders: FEMA; Review Board; state and federal dam safety officials

6. Continue to sponsor technical research on the consequences of dam failures, i.e., estimating failure flows.

   Stakeholders: FEMA; Review Board; PREP

7. Continue to expand ASDSO workshops for dam owners and emergency responders.

   Stakeholders: FEMA; ASDSO

8. Consider the establishment of national, multi-state, and multi-county workshops for educating dam owners and their engineers and local officials on emergency action planning and exercises.

   Stakeholders: FEMA; Review Board; ASDSO

C. Finding #3: The EAP Document Can Be Improved

The Task Group found that the EAP document often is overly detailed and not user-friendly. Task Group members found that emergency responders can be overwhelmed by the length of the EAP and the number of EAP's required for dams in their jurisdiction.

Recommendations:

1. Update the *Federal Guidelines for Dam Safety: Emergency Action Planning for Dam Owners* (FEMA 64).

   Stakeholders: Interagency Committee on Dam Safety (ICODS); Review Board

2. If appropriate, the EAP should address the impacts of upstream and downstream failures.

   Stakeholders: State and federal dam safety officials; dam owners

3. Continue to support the development of model EAP's that can most efficiently and effectively address the needs of the dams by their hazard classification, such as the work being done by ASDSO and the NRCS.

Stakeholders: FEMA; Review Board; ASDSO

D. Finding #4: Non-Federal High-Hazard Potential Classification Dams Must be Mapped for Dam Breach

Although 40 percent of non-federal high-hazard potential classification dams have EAP's, inundation maps are not required for some of these EAP's. The Task Group found that all non-federal high-hazard potential classification dams must be mapped for dam breach in order to save lives and reduce casualties from dam failure. Pending legislation (H.R. 4973) for the FEMA Flood Map Modernization Program provides for the mapping of a separate layer for areas downstream of dams. There is $300 million a year proposed for the mapping of additional hazards from Fiscal Year (FY) 2008 through 2012.

Recommendations:

1. Establish a Review Board Task Group to develop a standard methodology for mapping areas downstream of dams for use in FEMA's Flood Map Modernization Program. The Task Group should include representatives from FEMA's Flood Map Modernization Program and other stakeholder groups.

Stakeholders: FEMA; Review Board; PREP

2. Once a standard methodology is developed, encourage the application of the standard methodology for mapping areas downstream of dams.

Stakeholders: FEMA; Review Board

3. Consider the use of other funding sources for the development of breach maps (*see page 11 on funding sources.*)

E. Finding #5: Some States Do Not Require EAP's for High-Hazard Potential Classification Dams

The Task Group found a disparity in existing state laws and regulations related to EAP's for high-hazard potential classification dams. For 2004, the DSPMT shows that 22 states have regulations that require a dam owner of a high-or significant-hazard potential classification dam to prepare, update, and periodically test an EAP. [4] Thirteen states do not have this requirement, or only partially implement the requirement, i.e., high-hazard potential classification dams only or preparation of an EAP but not periodic exercises. Sixteen states did not respond to the question posed by the DSPMT. Of the 8,313 state-regulated high-hazard potential dams listed in the currently published National Inventory of Dams (NID), 726 (9 percent) are indicated as not requiring an EAP.

Recommendations:

1. The Review Board strongly recommends that states adopt regulations that require the development of EAP's for high-hazard potential classification dams. One mechanism for conveying the Review

---

[4] The annual ASDSO survey question on state requirements for EAP's does not differentiate between high-and significant-hazard dams.

Board's recommendation is a transmittal letter from the DHS to State Governors of the biennial report on the National Dam Safety Program for FY 2003-2004.

Stakeholders: Review Board; DHS, FEMA

2. Regardless of state law or regulation, dam owners should prepare EAP's for high-hazard potential dams.

Stakeholders: Dam owners

3. States should provide the DSPMT with comprehensive, accurate, and current data on emergency action planning for dams. (There may be local/county requirements related to EAP's.)

Stakeholders: State dam safety officials; ASDSO; DSMPT

4. The DHS Government Coordinating Council (GCC) and Sector Coordinating Council (SCC) for the Dam Sector should incorporate EAP's as an integral part of any security and protection planning efforts, and as complementary elements of the corresponding Security Plans.

Stakeholders: PREP; FEMA

5. Communities should be made aware that the Community Rating System (CRS) provides points for EAP's for high-hazard potential classification dams, and that having these EAP's and exercising them will increase points toward reducing their Federal Flood Insurance Rates.

Stakeholders: FEMA; ASDSO; ASFPM

6. Require dam owners to develop and implement EAP's before initiating construction contracts for new high-hazard potential classification dams or for the rehabilitation of existing high-hazard potential classification dams.

Stakeholders: Policymakers

7. Pending dam rehabilitation legislation (S. 2444) would authorize grants up to $100 million a year to states (FY 2008-2010) to upgrade deficient public dams. A requirement should be added that would require that an EAP be in place before any grant funds are spent on a construction project.

Stakeholders: Policymakers

F. Finding #6: There are Limited Funds for Emergency Action Planning for Dams

The Task Group found that funding is a primary constraint on the institutionalization of emergency action planning for dams.

Recommendations:

1. The Task Group will develop a summary for dissemination to state and local authorities of grant funds that may be used for the development and exercise of EAP's. The summary will include the following funding sources, among others:

- National Floodplain Management Grants

- State Grants Funds under National Dam Safety Program

- DHS Grant Programs: Buffer Zone Protection Program. The Buffer Zone Protection Program (BZPP) is a DHS-administered grant program to help secure and protect facilities by providing grant funds to local law enforcement to increase "buffer zone" security around critical infrastructure/key resources. The "buffer zone" is the area outside a facility that can be used by an adversary to conduct surveillance or launch an attack.

- Funding under S. 2444 that may result in many additional states gaining EAP requirement authority.

  Stakeholders: FEMA; Review Board; PREP

2. Identify opportunities for incorporating EAP's into the requirements of existing grant programs, such as the Hazard Mitigation Program Grants (HMPG), and new grant programs.

   Stakeholders: FEMA; Review Board; PREP

APPENDIX A: STRATEGIES AND BEST PRACTICES FOR EMERGENCY ACTION PLANNING

The Task Group on Emergency Action Planning and Response (Task Group) considered a number of issues affecting emergency action planning for dams. This section presents strategies and best practices to address these issues, with the goal of significantly increasing the number of Emergency Action Plans (EAP's) for state-regulated high-hazard potential dams.

A. Institutional Barriers to Effective Communication

It is essential that state dam safety officials and dam owners develop partnerships with emergency managers of the various levels of government who would be involved in an emergency incident at dams within their jurisdictions. Some states and federal agencies have had good success in working with their emergency management counterparts, as well as working with other dam owners in developing emergency response procedures and performing joint emergency exercises.

B. Best Processes for Communication

The primary means of notification to the public is the National Weather Service (NWS). The NWS has the Congressional mandate for issuing flood warnings, which includes dam failure. The NWS has a well established warning infrastructure that includes access to the Emergency Alert System (the successor to the Emergency Broadcast System-EBS), Weather Radio network, and Internet-based mechanisms. The other principle link is the downstream "warning points." This is usually a joint first responder dispatch center or sheriff's office. In general, this is where the local 9-1-1 center is located.

In cooperation with the Department of Homeland Security (DHS), the NWS radio warning system is now a major means of warning the public of selected security issues. Dam failures certainly are major security issues. Any standard EAP should include the NWS as a first point of notification so that the information may be put out over the NWS warning system.

Communication with non-governmental organizations (NGO's), such as the American Red Cross, should be through the local and state Emergency Operations Center (EOC). Coordination with the media should be through a Joint Information Center (JIC).

Consideration also should be given to communication with residents and businesses in close proximity to dams that must be notified immediately in the event of a dam failure. Procedures should be in place to ensure that it is possible to notify nearby residents before they would be impacted by high flows. Site-specific warning systems, such as sirens, in conjunction with public education programs, may be necessary. If agreed to by emergency management agencies, dam personnel may need to take on notification responsibilities for those structures.

C. Benefits of a Centralized Approach to Decision-Making

In theory, centralized decision-making should occur, especially in an incident without any warning time, such as an earthquake. The EAP should identify immediate actions that should be taken at the dam if there are indications that a loading condition may lead to a breach.

The Joint Incident Command is a management system that was developed by fire and rescue first responders. DHS has adopted this system to manage all major disasters in the United States when several government agencies and organizations have responsibilities for responding to the disaster. The application of a Joint Incident Command system begins with the arrival of the first official on the disaster scene who becomes the Incident Commander and is responsible to initiate the Joint Incident Command until this responsibility is passed on to the next Incident Commander.

D. Responsibilities of Emergency Responders

It is the responsibility of the dam owner to develop an EAP for high-hazard potential dams and to exercise it. In turn, it is the responsibility of emergency managers to take the plan and apply it to their jurisdictions. Dam awareness and operations must be a priority for emergency managers at all levels. The need for all concerned to become familiar with dam operations and safety constraints is paramount.

One federal agency identifies five components to its dam safety emergency management program: detection, decision-making, notification, warning, and evacuation. The first three components (detection, decision-making, and notification actions) are the responsibility of the dam owner/operator. The last two components (warning and evacuation) are the responsibility of the downstream public safety agencies.

The following is an excerpt from an emergency management standards and directive:

Downstream Warning and Evacuation. Area/Regional Offices will work with the dam operating entity to:

A. Maintain a redundant means to timely communicate, *e.g.*, primary telephone with back-up radio) with emergency management officials.

B. Provide inundation maps and other appropriate information and offer technical assistance, specifically staff support for interpretation of technical information, to local emergency management officials for their development of, or revisions to, their dam specific Emergency Operations Plans (EOP's).

C. Coordinate annually with appropriate federal, state, and/or local emergency management officials to:

(1) Support local efforts to attain and maintain the capability to effectively warn and evacuate persons placed at risk by operational releases or dam failure.
(2) Ensure that the local dam-specific EOP response procedures are properly linked to the corresponding notification procedures in EAP's.
(3) Encourage and participate in joint exercises involving dams, when such occur.
(4) Document all coordination efforts with emergency management officials for future reference purposes.
(5) Ensure that responsible operating entities carry out these activities similar to other delegated Operation & Maintenance (O&M) activities.

D. If appropriate, provide a copy of the Local Warning and Evacuation Plan Prototype, which is in the Emergency Planning and Exercise Guidelines, to local emergency management officials to support their efforts in development of their dam specific EOP's.

The following is a list of responsibilities developed by one State's emergency management officials:

- Dam Owners/Operators
  - Identification of emergency
  - Notifications
  - Implementation of repairs
  - Security and technical assistance on site

- Local Emergency Management and Local Responders
  - Public warning
  - Possible evacuation
  - Shelter plan activated
  - Rescue and recovery
  - SOE Declaration
  - Termination of Emergency Status

- County Emergency Management
  - Warning and notifications to affected municipalities of emergency condition
  - Assist municipalities of emergency responsibilities
  - Termination of off-site emergency condition

- State Emergency Management
  - Provide assistance to affected area when requested
  - Coordinate specialized assistance
  - Notify appropriate state agencies

13

E. Most Effective Procedures for Notification

As discussed above, the primary means of notification to the public should be the NWS.

The EAP provides the blueprint for notifying responsible downstream emergency management authorities of the emergency situation.

- Purpose of the EAP
  - To help save lives and reduce property damage in the event of an actual dam failure or other uncontrollable water release

- Functions of the EAP
  - To identify emergency conditions and classifications
  - Early notification process to local/county/State Government
  - Inundation mapping of potentially impacted areas

- Sections of a Standard EAP
  - Emergency notification
  - Emergency detection and evaluation

❖ Roles and responsibilities
❖ Emergency preparedness
❖ Inundation mapping
❖ Appendices (training, exercises, plan updates)

- Recommended notification procedure is the Call Tree (the most popular type of notification list)
  ❖ Visual notification list, easy to follow
  ❖ Notification time test-this chart can be easily tested to see how long it takes to notify residents and officials.
  ❖ If one persons fails to contact someone, the whole system could fail
  ❖ Must be constantly updated

F. Back-Up Procedures for Notification

The key in this area is "interoperable communications systems." For example, in some operating areas, local jurisdictions have exchanged "talk groups" to talk to each other over radio systems. Dam safety agencies also work with local emergency management agencies to have amateur radio personnel report information to the dam site via voice, video, and packet (alpha/numeric) and from the dam site to the downstream EOC's.

The following are strategies recommended by one State's emergency management officials:

- Direct Dial
  ❖ + Peace of mind - direct contact with down stream residents/officials
  ❖ - Only works if residents are home and within phone range
  ❖ - Takes time
  ❖ - Will not work if there are phone/power outages

- Reverse 911 (becoming very popular where available)
  ❖ + Can make multiple calls at one time to certain locations
  ❖ - Similar to direct dialing, residents/officials need to be near their phone

- Door-to-Door Notifications
  ❖ + Accountability - tracking system (who is leaving, staying, not home, etc.)
  ❖ - Time consuming

- Weather Radio (provided by the dam owner to downstream residents)
  ❖ + Quick distribution of severe weather information for a particular area as well as emergency notifications
  ❖ + Residents below dams usually live in rural valleys where radio coverage may be spotty or non existent
  ❖ - Programming these radios may be difficult for some residents, causing the system to be unsuccessfully programmed
  ❖ - Only works if residents/officials leave their radios turned on

Note: The model used by some: Model R-1650, 7-Channel S.A.M.E. Weather Radio from Reecom Electronics.

- The Emergency Alert System (EAS)
  - ❖ + Can send alerts and messages out to multiple areas via television and radio
  - ❖ - Only works if residents/officials television or radio is turned on
  - ❖ - Satellite television subscribers may not get alerts

- State Police Information Network
  - ❖ + Allows quick distribution of event messages to surrounding law enforcement agencies as well as Warning Points

- Sirens
  - ❖ + Allows for quick notifications
  - ❖ - Maintenance
  - ❖ - Dependability - can they be heard in all areas?
  - ❖ - Residents may not understand siren tones

G. Periodic Exercise of EAP's

Exercises of EAP's should be a management "report card" activity. For example, at one federal agency, dam safety exercises are a check-list item in the annual dam safety report. One federal agency also has a "Standard and Directive." This document requires tabletop exercises and functional exercises on a recurring 3-year cycle, which is intended to coincide with the periodic and comprehensive dam safety inspection schedule.

H. Interagency Coordination of EAP Exercises

The following are steps to improve the interagency coordination of EAP exercises:

1. Have all participating agencies come up with long-term schedule of EAP functional exercises (preferably 2-5 years).

2. Create a new database or modify an existing database, such as the National Inventory of Dams (NID), with information about the long-term schedule of exercises. Include the following data for each dam:

- Dam Name
- NATDAM number
- State
- River Name
- River Basin
- River mile
- Latitude/Longitude
- Agency with jurisdiction
- Date of last Functional Exercise
- Scheduled date for next Functional Exercise

3. If available, use GIS to plot maps showing dams with scheduled exercises. If inundation maps are digitized, this information could also be applied to the GIS system.

4. Determine if two or more dams that are under different jurisdictions have scheduled exercises and are in close proximity with each other.

5. Determine if dams with scheduled exercises are in close proximity with other high-hazard potential dams under different jurisdictions that have not had a recent exercise.

6. Check if the failure of the dams would affect similar populations and/or emergency management agencies. This can be verified by reviewing EAP notification flow charts and inundation maps or the GIS maps to see if two dams are upstream of the same city.

7. Agencies discuss and come to an agreement that two or more dams are good candidates for a combined exercise.

8. Agencies should contact the dam owners and discuss if they would be interested in combining exercises to form a joint exercise. If necessary, the exercises should be re-scheduled to align with a combined exercise.

I. Participation of Appropriate Personnel in EAP Exercises

The following are steps that can be taken to ensure the participation of appropriate personnel in EAP exercises:

1. Hand-deliver EAP updates to the agencies. This provides an opportunity to develop a relationship with agency personnel and verify that they have a current version of the EAP.

2. Meet face-to-face with the agencies to discuss exercises. Explain that the personnel involved in an actual emergency, those who are responsible for coordination and implementation of the EAP, should participate in EAP exercises.

3. When it is not possible to meet with the agencies, call them.

4. Obtain the agencies' input on exercises. If possible, allow the agencies to introduce other emergencies that could occur at the time of the dam failure to test their capabilities to respond to several incidents at one time.

5. Have regulatory agency staff involved. Regulatory staff could accompany dam owners to face-to-face meetings with the agencies and emphasize the importance of their participation in an EAP exercise.

6. Give the agencies a tour of the dam facility.

7. Feed them. Provide coffee and doughnuts in the morning and lunch, following the post-exercise evaluation.

8. Schedule the exercise when the major participants can attend. When dealing with a large number of volunteers, it may be necessary to schedule exercises at night.

Some agencies have had good success in arranging for appropriate agencies and personnel to participate in EAP exercises. There have, however, been occasions where agencies that were invited to exercises have not participated. This usually is because of scheduling conflicts. It is also a good idea to use a deliberate EAP exercise design process that includes representatives of key agencies that would be involved in an incident at one of its facilities on its exercise design teams. This pre-exercise involvement can increase the participation in the exercises.

J. Action Undertaken to Implement Homeland Security Presidential Directive/HSPD-5, Subject: Management of Domestic Incidents (National Incident Management System-NIMS) with EAPs

The purpose of HSPD-5 is "To enhance the ability of the United States to manage domestic incidents by establishing a single, comprehensive national incident management system." A common scenario would include an incident management team at a dam that would be managing the water operations and any static or dynamic problems at the facility while the downstream public safety agencies would be implementing their own incident command system to deal with warning of the population a risk, evacuation of people in the inundation area, traffic control in the impacted area, and sheltering of evacuees. The key is that a large geographic area that may be impacted by high operational releases or a dam failure will probably require the establishment of multiple incident command posts in the disaster area. Given this scenario, representatives of the dam operating agency and public safety agencies need to work together in either a "unified command" or under the doctrine of an "area command authority" under the Incident Command System.

Personnel from the dam operating agency must be part of the overall incident management structure if their facility is involved in the emergency, *i.e.*, making high operational releases or when the potential exists for a dam failure. How that is done must be determined on a site-by-site basis, after reviewing authorities and jurisdictions, in discussions with all agencies involved on the best method for incident management. This incident management strategy then needs to be documented in the EAP.

APPENDIX B: STATUS OF STATE EMERGENCY ACTION PLANNING

The U.S. Army Corps of Engineers (USACE), Dam Safety Program Management Tools (DSPMT), has provided a detailed description of the current status of emergency action planning by the states. The information is drawn from responses provided by the states to the combined Review Board/Association of State Dam Safety Officials (ASDSO) questions in 2005 for the 2004 reporting year, and from updated inventory information to the National Inventory of Dams (NID) provided in 2005/2006.

This section discusses the legislative authorities claimed by the states in performing emergency action planning and response, implementation of those authorities in state regulations, and state regulatory agency and dam owner success in performance and compliance with those regulations in the generation of EAP's for high-hazard potential dams.

There are two questions asked by the National Dam Safety Review Board (Review Board) related to emergency action planning and response. The first question, shown below, relates to emergency response in the event of a dam failure or imminent dam failure.

I. *A system of emergency procedures to be used if a Dam or the failure of the Dam is imminent.*

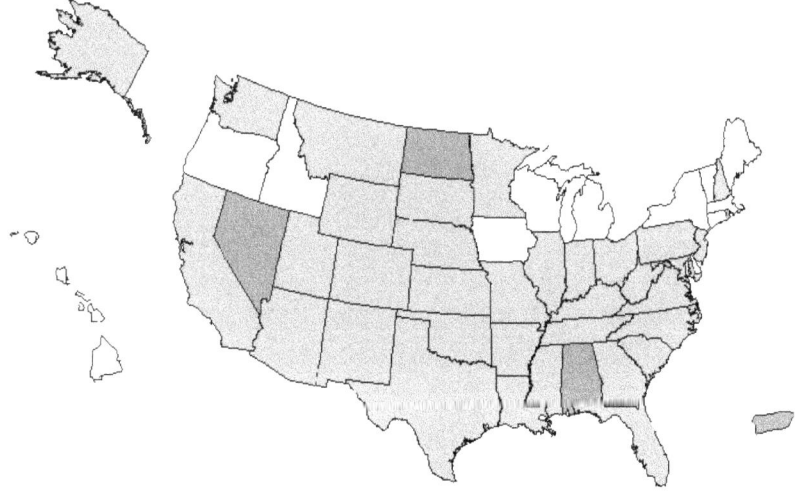

Figure 1
Source: DSPMT

The 34 states shown in green indicate that they have the authority and procedures for responding to emergency situations. The five states shown in red indicate that they do not. The 12 states shown in white did not respond to the question.

The second Review Board question, shown below in three parts, relates to the authority to perform hazard potential classification (to identify high-hazard potential classification dams) and to perform inundation mapping (an important part of the recommended EAP).

J. *An identification of:*

　1. *Each Dam the failure of which could reasonably be expected to endanger human life.*
　2. *The maximum area that could be flooded if the Dam failed.*
　3. *Necessary public facilities that would be affected by the flooding.*

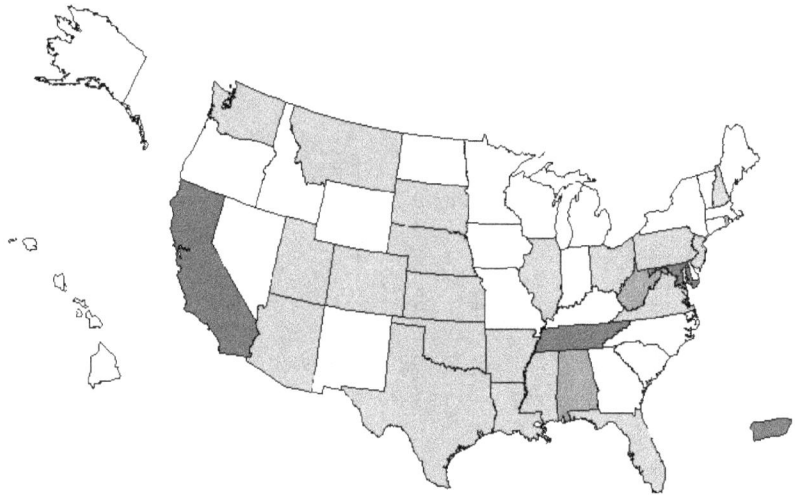

Figure 2
Source: DSPMT

The 21 states, shown in green, indicate that they have all authorities for both hazard potential classification and inundation mapping. The four states, shown in blue, have the legislative authority for two of the three authorities, *i.e.*, hazard potential classification and one of the inundation mapping authorities. The 12 states shown in yellow have the legislative authority for hazard potential classification only, no inundation mapping. The three states shown in red have neither the authority for hazard potential classification nor for inundation mapping. The 11 states shown in white did not respond to the Review Board question for the 2004 reporting period.

It is important to note that the legislative authority to develop or require the development of EAP's is not one of the 12 legislative authorities recommended by the Review Board. The development of EAP's is implemented within the regulations of the state regulatory agencies. There are two questions, shown below, which are asked by ASDSO regarding requirements for EAP's within the regulations of the states.

Does your State do the following? (yes/no):

1. State requires a dam owner of a high or significant hazard potential dam to prepare, update and periodically test an Emergency Action Plan (CRS Credit Point 8)?

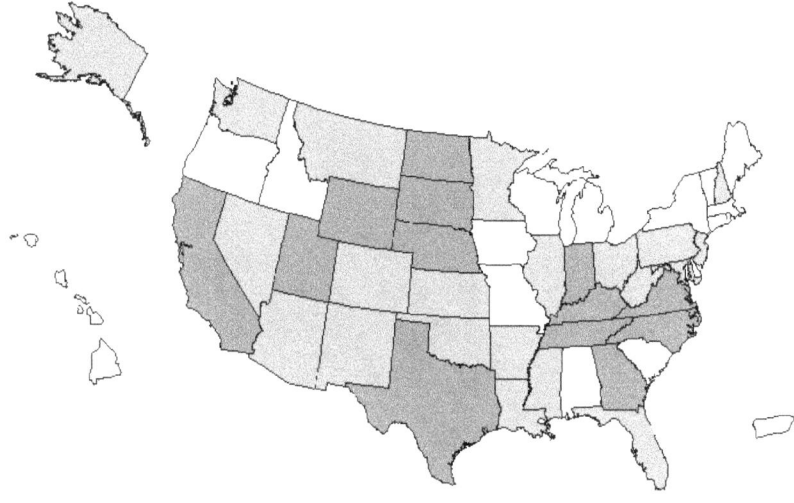

Figure 3
Source: DSPMT

The 22 states shown in green indicate that their regulations require a dam owner of a high-or significant-hazard potential classification dam to prepare, update, and periodically test an EAP. The 13 states shown in red do not have this requirement, or only partially implement the requirement, i.e., high-hazard potential classification dams only or preparation of an EAP but not to periodically test it. The 16 states shown in white did not respond to the question.

7. State requires the following basic elements in its Emergency Action Plans?

  a. Emergency notification flowchart and information?
  b. Statement of Purpose?
  c. Emergency detection, evaluation and action procedures?
  d. General responsibilities of each party?
  e. Preparedness actions?
  f. Inundation maps?
  g. Appendices of necessary documents?

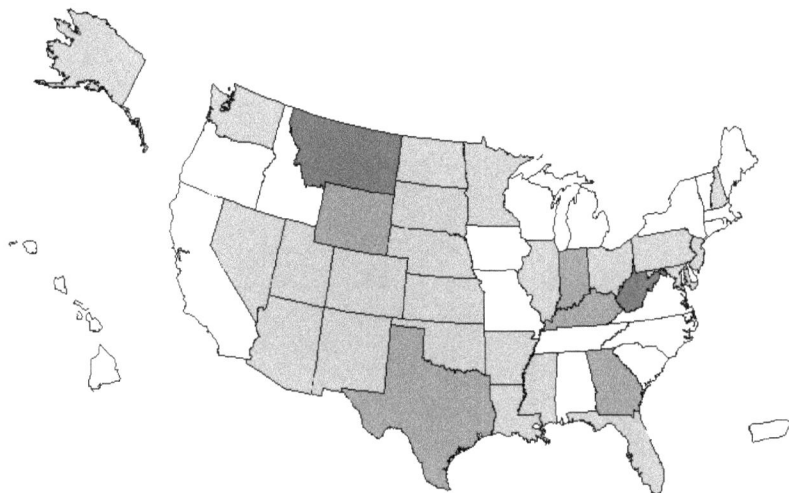

Figure 4
Source: DSPMT

The 24 states shown in green indicate that they require all 7 of the recommended basic elements in the EAP, including inundation maps. The two states shown in blue indicate that they require most (> 50 percent). The three states shown in yellow require some of the recommended elements. The five states shown in red require no elements of the recommended EAP, i.e., they do not require an EAP. The 17 states shown in white did not respond to the question.

This paragraph addresses state regulatory agency and dam owner success in performance and compliance with the state regulations for the generation of EAP's for high-hazard potential dams. The data used to generate the following figures is taken from the data collected in 2005/2006 from all 50 states and Puerto Rico for the update to the NID. This section shows three figures, the state-regulated high-hazard potential dams with EAP's, the ones without EAP's, and the ones for which an EAP is not required.

Non-Federal State-Regulated High-Hazard Potential Dams with EAP's (4,057 dams)

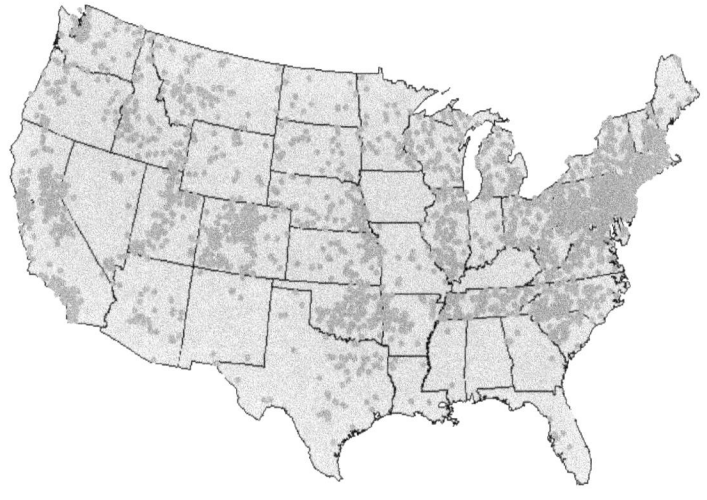

Figure 5
Source: DSPMT

Non-Federal State-Regulated High-Hazard Potential Dams without EAP's (3,356 dams)

Figure 6
Source: DSPMT

The states with lots of dots in the top figure but very few in the lower figure have a high completion percentage of high-hazard potential dams with EAP's.

It is interesting to note that there are some states with very few dots in either the upper or lower figure. This would indicate a lack of high-hazard potential dams either with or without EAP's. Examples include Georgia, Kentucky, and Alabama. Alabama does not have state-regulated dams because it does not have a legislated dam safety program. The reason for the other states is illustrated in the following figure, which shows the locations of state-regulated high-hazard potential dams in which EAP's are not required.

Non-Federal State-Regulated High-Hazard Potential Dams Not Requiring EAP's (726 dams)

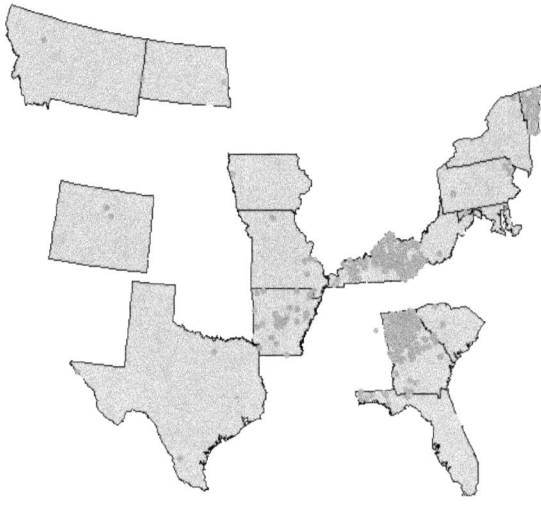

Figure 7
Source: DSPMT

EAP's are not required for the 726 non-federal state-regulated high-hazard potential classification dams shown in this figure.

In summary, the states' dam inventories contain 8,313 total non-federal state-regulated high-hazard potential classification dams. Of these, 4,057 (49 percent) have EAP's, 3,356 (40 percent) do not, and 726 (9 percent) do not require one. The states have been providing information regarding the number of state-regulated high-hazard potential classification dams with EAP's to the Review Board since 1998 in their State Evaluation Criteria reports. The following figure shows the trend in this data:

State Regulated High Hazard Potential Dams with an EAP

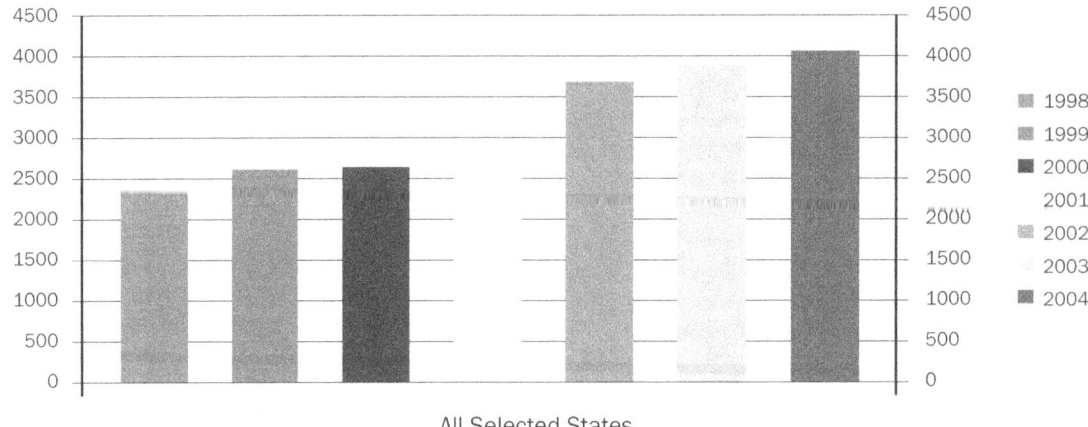

All Selected States

Figure 8
Source: DSPMT

This data is in very close agreement with the data provided in the most recent update of the NID, *i.e.*, 4,113 dams with EAP's from the Review Board report for 2004 versus 4,057 dams with EAP's from the 2005/2006 NID update. The EAP completion percentage trend is shown below:

State Regulated High Hazard Potential Dams with an EAP

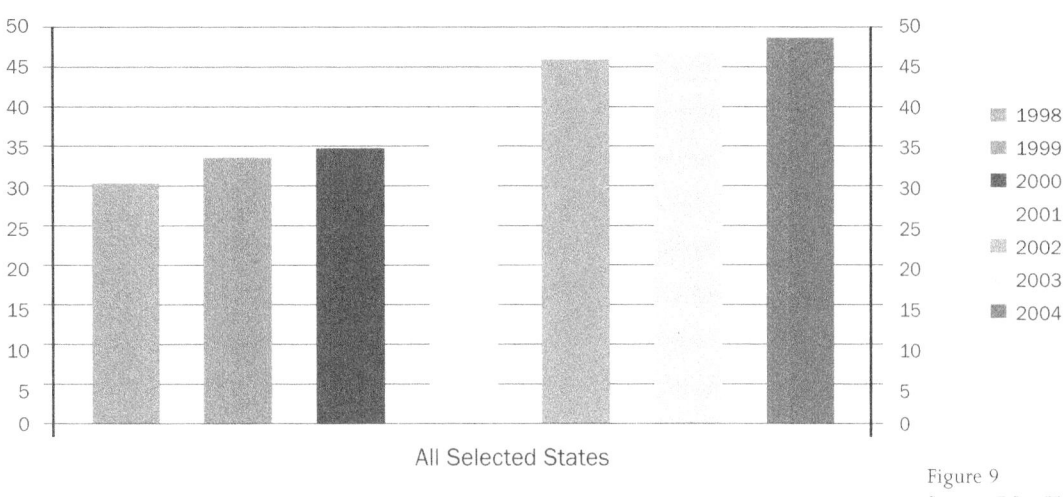

All Selected States

Figure 9
Source: DSPMT

Although this trend shows significant improvement in the number of EAP's developed for high-hazard potential dams since 1998, there is still room for improvement.

APPENDIX C: NDSP PERFORMANCE MEASURE ON EMERGENCY ACTION PLANNING

Performance Evaluation System

Performance Measure Specifications Form

State Performance Measure Identifier #3: Emergency Action Planning

Strategic Goal	Goal B: Reduce the risk associated with dams.
Strategic Objective	Achieve 100 percent compliance for EAPs for high-hazard potential dams.
Period of Performance	☐ Short-term (< 2 years) ☐ Intermediate (2–5 years) ☒ Long-term (> 5 years)

Specifications of the Performance Measure:

Outcome Measure	Number of high-hazard potential dams with current EAPs.
Definition	**"High-hazard potential dam"** is defined as a dam whose failure or mis-operation will probably cause loss of human life. **"Current"** is defined as a periodic (at least annual) review of the EAP to assess its workability and efficiency, i.e., timeliness of implementation, and to improve weak areas. Changes that may frequently require revision and update of an EAP include changes in personnel and changes in communications systems. A review also should be made of any changes to the dam and/or floodplain as this may affect the information on the inundation maps. The states report this data annually to the DSPMT. The federal agencies collect the data annually and report the data on a biennial basis for the report to Congress on the National Dam Safety Program.

Data Source	States; Federal agencies; DSPMT.
Frequency of Measurements	Annual, with baseline data established at the end of Calendar Year (CY) 2005.
Baseline Measurement	States, Federal agencies, DSPMT data for CY 2005.
Target Measurement(s) and Associated Timeframe(s)	CY 2006: CY 2007: CY 2008: CY 2009: CY 2010:
Other	Targets set annually, based on appropriated funding. The National Dam Safety Review Board considered including significant-hazard potential dams under this performance measure but decided to defer their inclusion because of the need to focus on high-hazard potential dams. Significant-hazard potential dams will be added in the future when a target percentage of high-hazard potential dams (80 to 90 percent) has been reached.

APPENDIX D: TASK GROUP ROSTER

National Dam Safety Review Board
Task Group on Emergency Action Planning and Response

September 2006

Task Group Chair
Gene Zeizel
Assessment and Planning Section
Risk Analysis Branch
Mitigation Division
DHS/FEMA
gene.zeizel@dhs.gov

Members
Larry Caldwell
U.S. Department of Agriculture
Natural Resources Conservation Service
larry.caldwell@ok.usda.gov

James Demby
U.S. Department of Agriculture
Forest Service
jdemby@fs.fed.us

Thomas Donaldson
National Oceanic and Atmospheric Administration
National Weather Service
thomas.donaldson@noaa.gov

Mark Ferrari
Regional Director
State of New York
SEMO Region II
mark.ferrari@semo.state.ny.us

Mike Grounds
Beacon Resources
mike@riversrus.com

Rita Henry
Assessment and Planning Section
Risk Analysis Branch
Mitigation Division
DHS/FEMA
rita.henry@dhs.gov

Bill Irwin
National Design Engineer
U.S. Department of Agriculture
Natural Resources Conservation Service
Bill.Irwin@wdc.usda.gov

Don Kirkwood
Mine Waste and Geotechnical Engineering Division
Pittsburgh Safety & Health Technical Center
Mine Safety and Health Administration
kirkwood.donald@dol.gov

Steven Knecht
State of Montana
Response Coordinator
Montana Disaster & Emergency Services
sknecht@mt.gov

Enrique Matheu
Department of Homeland Security
Office of Infrastructure Protection
Enrique.matheu@dhs.gov

Tony Niles
U.S. Army Corps of Engineers
Anthony.R.Niles@erdc.usace.army.mil

Ken Rakestraw
Department of State
International Boundary and Water Commission
kenrakestraw@ibwc.state.gov

Paul Shannon
Federal Energy Regulatory Commission
paul.shannon@ferc.gov

Frederick Sharrocks
Chief, Assessment and Planning Section
Risk Analysis Branch
Mitigation Division
DHS/FEMA
frederick.sharrocks@dhs.gov

Laurence Siroky
Chief, Water Operations
Montana Department of Natural Resources
  and Conservation
lsiroky@mt.gov

Kenneth E. Smith
Assistant Director
Indiana Department of Natural Resources
Division of Water
kesmith@dnr.in.gov

David Snyder
Federal Energy Regulatory Commission
david.snyder@ferc.gov

Grant Sorensen
Department of the Interior
Bureau of Reclamation
gsorensen@do.usbr.gov

Don Taussig
Department of the Interior
Bureau of Reclamation
dtaussig@do.usbr.gov

Gus Tjoumas
Director, Division of Dam Safety and Inspections
Federal Energy Regulatory Commission
gus.tjoumas@ferc.gov

Kelvin Wu
Chief, Mine Waste and Geotechnical
  Engineering Division
Dam Safety Officer
Pittsburgh Safety & Health Tech Center
Mine Safety and Health Administration
wu.kelvinkekang@dol.gov